The State and Pattern of
HEALTH
Information Technology
Adoption

Kateryna Fonkych

Roger Taylor

Sponsored by Cerner Corporation, General Electric, Hewlett-Packard, Johnson & Johnson, and Xerox

RAND | HEALTH

The research described in this report was conducted within RAND Health and sponsored by a consortium of private companies, including Cerner Corporation, General Electric, Hewlett-Packard, Johnson & Johnson, and Xerox.

Library of Congress Cataloging-in-Publication Data

Fonkych, Kateryna.
    The state and pattern of health information technology adoption /
Kateryna Fonkych, Roger Taylor.
        p. cm.
        "MG-409."
        Includes bibliographical references.
        ISBN 0-8330-3847-8 (pbk. : alk. paper)
        1. Health services administration—Information technology. 2. Medical care—
Information technology.
        [DNLM: 1. Public Health Informatics—trends. 2. Medical Informatics
Applications. WA 26.5 F673s 2005] I. Taylor, Roger, MD. II. Rand Corporation.
III.Title.

    RA971.23.F66 2005
    362.1'028—dc22

                                                                        2005021867

The RAND Corporation is a nonprofit research organization providing objective analysis and effective solutions that address the challenges facing the public and private sectors around the world. RAND's publications do not necessarily reflect the opinions of its research clients and sponsors.

RAND® is a registered trademark.

A profile of RAND Health, abstracts of its publications, and ordering information can be found on the RAND Health home page at www.rand.org/health.

Cover design by Barbara Angell Caslon

Published 2005 by the RAND Corporation
1776 Main Street, P.O. Box 2138, Santa Monica, CA 90407-2138
1200 South Hayes Street, Arlington, VA 22202-5050
201 North Craig Street, Suite 202, Pittsburgh, PA 15213-1516
RAND URL: http://www.rand.org/
To order RAND documents or to obtain additional information, contact
Distribution Services: Telephone: (310) 451-7002;
Fax: (310) 451-6915; Email: order@rand.org

Preface

It is widely believed that broad adoption of Electronic Medical Record Systems (EMR-S) will lead to significant healthcare savings, reduce medical errors, and improve health, effectively transforming the U.S. healthcare system. Yet, adoption of EMR-S has been slow and appears to lag the effective application of information technology (IT) and related transformations seen in other industries, such as banking, retail, and telecommunications. In 2003, RAND Health began a broad study to better understand the role and importance of EMR-S in improving health and reducing healthcare costs, and to help inform government actions, if any, that could maximize EMR-S benefits and increase their use.

This report provides the technical details and results on the current state and dynamics of clinical Health Information Technology (HIT) adoption in inpatient and outpatient settings. In addition, it describes how a HIT-adoption pattern varies across different types of providers and relates market factors and parent-system characteristics to HIT-adoption level. The results of this report can be used to derive policies on HIT adoption. Related documents are as follows:

- Richard Hillestad, James Bigelow, Anthony Bower, Federico Girosi, Robin Meili, Richard Scoville, and Roger Taylor, "Can Electronic Medical Record Systems Transform Healthcare? Potential Health Benefits, Savings, and Costs," *Health Affairs,* Vol. 24, No. 5, September 14, 2005.
- Roger Taylor, Anthony Bower, Federico Girosi, James Bigelow, Kateryna Fonkych, and Richard Hillestad, "Promoting Health Information Technology: Is There a Case for More-Aggressive Government Action?" *Health Affairs,* Vol. 24, No. 5, September 14, 2005.
- James Bigelow et al., "Technical Executive Summary in Support of 'Can Electronic Medical Record Systems Transform Healthcare?' and 'Promoting Health Information Technology'," *Health Affairs,* Web Exclusive, September 14, 2005.

- James Bigelow, Kateryna Fonkych, Constance Fung, and Jason Wang, *Analysis of Healthcare Interventions That Change Patient Trajectories,* Santa Monica, Calif.: RAND Corporation, MG-408-HLTH, 2005.
- Federico Girosi, Robin Meili, and Richard Scoville, *Extrapolating Evidence of Health Information Technology Savings and Costs,* Santa Monica, Calif.: RAND Corporation, MG-410-HLTH, 2005.
- Richard Scoville, Roger Taylor, Robin Meili, and Richard Hillestad, *How HIT Can Help: Process Change and the Benefits of Healthcare Information Technology,* Santa Monica, Calif.: RAND Corporation, TR-270-HLTH, 2005.
- Anthony G. Bower, *The Diffusion and Value of Healthcare Information Technology,* Santa Monica, Calif.: RAND Corporation, MG-272-HLTH, 2005.

The report should be of interest to healthcare IT professionals, other healthcare executives and researchers, and officials in the government responsible for health policy.

This work was sponsored by a generous consortium of private companies: Cerner Corporation, General Electric, Hewlett-Packard, Johnson & Johnson, and Xerox. A steering group headed by Dr. David Lawrence, a retired CEO of Kaiser Permanente, provided review and guidance throughout the project. The right to publish any results was retained by RAND. The research was conducted in RAND Health, a division of the RAND Corporation. A profile of RAND Health, abstracts of its publications, and ordering information can be found at www.rand.org/health.

Contents

Figures

Tables

Summary

Innovations in information technology (IT) have improved efficiency and quality in many industries. Healthcare has not been one of them. Although some administrative IT systems, such as those for billing, scheduling, and inventory management, are already in place in the healthcare industry, little adoption of clinical IT, such as Electronic Medical Record Systems (EMR-S) and Clinical Decision Support tools, has occurred. Government intervention has been called for to speed the adoption process for Health Information Technology (HIT), based on the widespread belief that its adoption, or diffusion, is too slow to be socially optimal.

In this report, we estimate the current level and pattern of HIT adoption in the different types of healthcare organizations, and we evaluate factors that affect this diffusion process. First, we make an effort to derive a population-wide adoption level of administrative and clinical HIT applications according to information in the Healthcare Information and Management Systems Society (HIMSS)-Dorenfest database (formerly the Dorenfest IHDS+TM Database, second release, 2004) and compare our estimates to alternative ones. We then attempt to summarize the current state and dynamics of HIT adoption according to these data and briefly review existing empirical studies on the HIT-adoption process. By comparing adoption rates across different types of healthcare providers and geographical areas, we help focus the policy agenda by identifying which healthcare providers lag behind and may need the most incentives to adopt HIT. Next, we employ regression analysis to separate the effects of the provider's characteristics and factors on adoption of Electronic Medical Records (EMR), Computerized Physician Order Entry (CPOE), and Picture Archiving Communications Systems (PACS), and compare the effects to findings in the literature.

The results of the analysis suggest high heterogeneity in HIT adoption, across HIT applications and types of providers, such as for-profit and non-profit hospitals. We discuss the hypotheses that explain our empirical findings and the forces behind HIT adoption, and we link hypotheses and forces to potential policy implications. Additional evaluation of HIT adoption at the level of healthcare systems, rather than their facilities, suggests the potential for system-based connectivity and future patterns of adoption.

Acronyms

AHA	American Hospital Association
CDR	Clinical Data Repository
CDS	Clinical Decision Support
CIO	Corporate Information Officer
CMS	Center for Medicare and Medicaid Services
CPOE	Computerized Physician Order Entry
CPR	Computerized Patient Records
DRG	diagnosis-related groups
EMR	Electronic Medical Record
EMR-S	Electronic Medical Record System
FTE	full-time equivalent (staff)
HCRIS	Healthcare Cost Report Information System
HHI	Hirschman-Herfidahl Index
HIMSS	Healthcare Information and Management Systems Society
HIS	hospital information systems
HIT	Health Information Technology
HMO	health maintenance organization
IHDS	integrated healthcare delivery system
IT	information technology
LOS	length of stay
MGMA	Medical Group Management Association
MRI	Medical Records Institute
MSA	metropolitan service areas
OCF	Open Clinical Foundation
PACS	Picture Archiving Communications System

POS   point of service
ROA   return on assets
ROI   return on investment
SJCRH   St. Jude Children's Research Hospital

CHAPTER ONE

Introduction and Review of the Literature

Introduction

The call for government intervention in the adoption process for Health Information Technology (HIT) is based on the widespread belief that the diffusion of HITs is too slow to be socially optimal. Innovations in information technology (IT) have improved the efficiency and quality of many industries; however, healthcare has yet to realize the tremendous potential of information technologies. It is widely perceived that, although some administrative IT systems, such as those for billing, scheduling, and inventory management, are already in place, little progress has occurred in adopting clinical IT, such as Electronic Medical Records Systems (EMR-S) and Clinical Decision Support tools, which would be the most useful systems for improving the quality, efficiency, and provision of more-integrated healthcare.

Few rigorous studies are available today that analyze the current level and speed of adoption of IT in different types of healthcare organizations, the factors that influence adoption, and expected diffusion patterns. The sparse literature that is available shows high heterogeneity in HIT-adoption behavior among healthcare providers with different characteristics. Thus, it is important to identify the characteristics and factors that influence adoption and to explain the forces behind them, to evaluate the effect of potential policies, and to suggest what the targets of such policies should be.

This report informs the HIT policy agenda by evaluating the current state and dynamics of the HIT-adoption process. It helps focus HIT policy initiatives by identifying which healthcare providers lag behind and need the most incentives to adopt HIT.

This basic exploratory analysis involves an objective evaluation of the current state of HIT adoption, to provide a rationale for the policies that stimulate HIT adoption, identify the target population for such policies, and build hypotheses about different factors that affect adoption and could be used to leverage policy. Our research is primarily based on the quantitative analysis of the HIT-adoption data, but the results are interpreted through our understanding of the relevant literature and qualitative information collected through site visits and interviews. As part of a larger HIT project, the RAND team visited 13 sites of healthcare organizations, including Trinity Healthcare System, Kaiser Permanente, Mayo Jacksonville Healthcare Center, and others, conducting open-ended interviews about their experience with HIT adoption. In addition, HIT experts, such as Dr. David Lawrence, and software vendors, such as Cerner and GE (General Electrics), were interviewed about their vision of HIT diffusion in the United States, its promises and pitfalls. The literature of interest includes empirical literature that analyzes HIT-adoption patterns among different healthcare providers, the reports on the surveys that ask about motivations and barriers for HIT adoption, and surveys of HIT adoption, which we used to compare with and augment our HIT-adoption estimates.

This chapter presents the background for our study, covering the empirical literature on HIT-adoption patterns and the factors that influence HIT adoption, which compares to our own research. Chapter Two presents our estimates of HIT adoption and augments them with estimates from alternative surveys. Chapter Three provides our analysis of HIT-adoption patterns, including univariate and multivariate analyses of the factors and characteristics that are related to HIT-adoption behavior. Chapter Four summarizes results and presents conclusions.

Literature Findings on Factors That Relate to HIT Adoption and the Influence of HIT

This brief overview of the literature on HIT and HIT adoption focuses on the factors that are related to HIT adoption and on the incentives that are driving the adoption process. The literature includes empirical evaluations of the effects of HIT on the performance of healthcare providers, which may drive their decisions on HIT adoption. The articles on these topics were found through the PubMed database and supplemental Internet searches.

Most studies have discovered a relationship between the financial well-being, size, and productivity of a healthcare facility and its level of HIT adoption. Nevertheless, it has always been difficult to assert the causality of this connection: Whether wealthy and more-productive hospitals can afford a strategic investment in HIT or whether HIT has positive effects on the hospital's performance. The "Most Wired" report (Solovy, 2001) by *Hospitals and Health Networks* and Deloitte Consulting shows that the "most-wired" hospitals—the most HIT-advanced, measured by HIT applications, connectivity among the components of HIT systems and among different types of providers in the organization, etc.—have better control of expenses and higher productivity, characteristics that were measured in terms of greater access to capital as a reflection of credit ratings. They are *more efficient* as measured by lower median expenses per discharge and *more productive* as measured by full-time equivalent staff (FTE) per adjusted occupied bed, paid hours per adjusted discharge, and net patient revenue per FTE.

Parente and Dunbar (2001) found that hospitals with integrated information systems have higher total margins and operating margins than those hospitals that do not have integrated information systems. However, their results were unable to disentangle the endogenous relationship between IT investment and profitability. They found that hospitals investing in healthcare IT had a higher total profit margin. However, it could also be that wealthier hospitals, with greater profits from operations and total assets, invested in IT. The multivariate regression analysis that Parente and Dunbar conducted showed no effect of HIT on the operating margin, suggesting that healthcare IT had little effect on performance and that the presence of IT could simply be a wealth effect.

Wang et al. (2002) studied the factors influencing hospital HIT adoption, using a sample of 1,441 hospitals located in metropolitan service areas (MSAs) in the United States in 1998. The results partially support the conclusion that managed care *turbulence*—the economic and market factors that cause competitive behavior from non–managed care organizations—positively influences the adoption of IT strategies in hospitals. Hospitals operating in a competitive environment are more likely than others to adopt IT. Hospitals with more staffed beds and more-complex services show a higher rate of adopting IT applications. The findings also show that hospitals with more information processing are more likely than others to adopt IT systems. Wang et al.'s results also show that hospitals affiliated with a multi-hospital system and those that are for-profit are more likely than others to have managerial IT applications. From a financial perspective, the findings indicate that hospitals with higher cash flows, revenues per bed, and operating margins are more likely than others to adopt healthcare IT systems.

Parente and Van Horn (2003) took a close look at differences in adoption behavior between for-profit and non-profit hospitals. They used panel data based on the Healthcare Information and Management Systems Society (HIMSS)-Dorenfest database and merged it with the American Hospital Association (AHA) and Healthcare Cost Report Information System (HCRIS) files, using a very broad definition for *clinical IT:* patient care systems. They found that the marginal effect of IT on for-profit hospital productivity is to reduce the number of days supplied, whereas, in non-profits, the marginal effect of IT is to increase the quantity of services supplied. Throughout most of the study period (1987–1998), they found a much higher rate of adoption of patient care IT systems in non-profit hospitals than in the for-profit hospitals. At a very general level, they did not find a relation between the financial performance of the hospital and adoption of the IT system.

The results of Parente and Van Horn's regression analysis on the factors of adoption suggest that for-profits are less likely to have an IT system, and, when they do, it is positively affected by the financial position of the hospital. Non-profits, on the other hand, are more likely to have a HIT system, to adopt the system earlier (negative coefficient on the time trend), and to make the investment when they have poor financial performance. Full-time equivalent employees per hospital bed (a crude measure of efficiency) was not related to whether the IT system was purchased. Hospitals with a higher Medicare case mix (sicker patients) were more likely to invest in IT. Parente and Van Horn also found that the higher the share of government-financed revenues (Medicare and Medicaid) is, the lower is the probability of clinical HIT adoption.

Parente and Van Horn also studied the effects of having clinical HIT in place on five different measures of efficiency: FTEs per hospital bed, length of stay (LOS), return on assets (ROA), case-mix-adjusted cost per patient-day, and case-mix-adjusted cost per discharge. Their study did not find an effect of IT on those dependent variables measuring efficiency in the non-profit hospitals. However, those variables are significant in the analysis of for-profit hospitals: IT *tenure*—the number of years since a HIT application was adopted—serves to reduce LOS and each case mix–adjusted cost measure, and it has a positive effect on ROA and FTEs per bed. These effects might be expected, given the for-profit orientation of the hospitals. In summary, IT appears to have a significant effect on multiple dimensions of for-profit hospital performance and no perceptible effect on non-profit hospital performance.

Parente and Van Horn also evaluated the effect of IT on hospital production capacity, measured as admissions, bed-days, and other services, allowing for the complementary and substitute effects that IT may have for labor and capital (measured, in this specification, as hospital beds). They found that IT increases the discharges of non-profit hospitals, which is consistent with non-profits' functional objective of maximizing the quantity of services provided within a community. For for-profit hospitals, IT has a negative effect on the number of patient bed-days and the costs associated with staffing beds for those days. Parente and Van Horn hypothesize that, in the world of managed care, for-profit hospitals are maximizing profits by using IT to reduce the number of inpatient hospital days. However, IT appears to have no statistically significant effect on the length of stay for non-profit hospitals and the volume of admissions within for-profit hospitals.

Borzekowski (2002a) examines the adoption of hospital information systems (HIS) in connection with the financing of health. The results indicate that state price regulations slowed the adoption of such systems during the 1970s. In contrast, hospitals increased their adoption of HIS in response to the implementation of Medicare's prospective payment system. The author suggests an explanation for the results: In the early years, these systems did not have the ability to save sufficient funds to justify their expense, and adopters—in particular, non-profit hospitals—were motivated by factors other than cost. By the early 1980s, this situation had changed: Hospitals with the greatest incentives to lower costs were now more likely to adopt such technologies. The finding about the initially causal effect of the diagnosis-related groups (DRG)-based Medicare prospective payment system may suggest a set of policies to promote HIT investment based on incentives for the hospital to improve its cost-efficiency.

Another study by Borzekowski (2002b) measures the impact of IT use on hospital operating costs during the late 1980s and early 1990s. He finds that the most thoroughly automated hospitals are associated with declining costs three and five years after adoption. At the application level, declining costs are associated with the adoption of some of the newest technologies, including systems designed for cost management, the administration of managed care contracts, and for both financial and clinical decision support. The association of cost declines that lagged IT and the cost patterns at the less-automated hospitals provide evidence of strong learning effects.

CHAPTER TWO

Estimates of Current HIT Adoption and of HIT Diffusion

In this chapter, we set out to derive a population-wide adoption level of administrative and clinical HIT applications according to information in the Healthcare Information and Management Systems Society (HIMSS)-Dorenfest database (formerly the Dorenfest IHDS+TM Database, second release, 2004) and compare our estimates with alternative estimates. We then attempt to summarize the current state and dynamics of HIT adoption according to these data and briefly review existing empirical studies on the HIT-adoption process.

Approach

There is no unique way to measure the adoption of a particular technology, because the definition of *adoption* varies by the stage in the adoption process and by the type of an adopting entity. Moreover, complex technologies, such as HIT software and hardware, have multiple unique functionalities, components, levels of sophistication, and generations, which make it difficult to identify any one particular technology at a specific point in time.

There are two major levels at which technology is adopted: the organization level, at which the HIT system is invested in and installed, and the clinical level, at which the intended users of the information system—doctors, nurses, administrative personnel, etc., within that organization—decide whether or not to incorporate that technology in their daily practice. In turn, healthcare organizations themselves may have several levels: a larger parent corporation (multi-hospital system or integrated healthcare delivery system [IHDS]), a hospital or ambulatory care center, and departments within a facility or individual physician offices. Technology adoption at the organization level may be more relevant for policy analysis, since it is the "organization" that makes an acquisition decision. The adoption of technology by the end users within an organization largely belongs in the sphere of organizational management. Nevertheless, the adoption process is related to both levels: an organization would likely invest in a technology only if its users are ready to accept the technology in the near future.

Because of data limitations and definitional problems, we focus our analysis on organization-level adoption: the healthcare facilities, their parent healthcare system, and affiliated physicians. We depend on general survey data to provide insights into use of the technology at the level of individual clinicians.

The adoption process takes some time and, nominally, starts with a contract to purchase a HIT application, system, or service, or an initiative for in-house development. After that, a HIT application is installed and integrated in some way with the organization's information system and infrastructure. It is hoped that doctors and other end users are trained to use the system and that the necessary changes in workflow and processes of care are initiated. As implementation progresses, the share of users of the new technology increases within a provider organization and the technology's functionality expands. Some organizations make use of Electronic Medical Records (EMR) and Computerized Physician Order Entry (CPOE) mandatory for everyone at once; other organizations allow for a gradual increase in adoption within the organization.

There is no strict definition of what *adopted* or *implemented* means in terms of the percentage of active HIT users among doctors or the depth of their use. Thus, a question in a HIT-adoption survey on whether an organization has implemented HIT could mean different things, ranging from "just have installed it" to "everybody is using it to its full potential."

To understand the differences in the adoption levels reported, it is useful to think of the organizational-adoption process in four major stages:

1. Deciding to invest and searching for options
2. Signing a contract to purchase a HIT system from a particular vendor (measured by "contracted" in our analysis)
3. Installing the system, so that it is ready to use (measured by "automated" in our analysis)
4. Learning how to use the system, integrating the system into the process of care, and broadening the use of the system's applicable functionalities. This stage may involve multiple levels of improvement in the use of the system, both in terms of the percentage of staff utilizing the system to support patient care and in the degree to which the organization takes advantage of HIT-enabled opportunities to restructure the way that care is delivered or that patients are integrated into the care process.

When comparing the estimates of HIT-adoption rates across the many published surveys, we must keep in mind that stages 2 and 3 can be documented and measured directly, whereas stages 1 and 4 are much more ambiguous. But when experts in the field observe HIT implementation, they are usually observing points in time during stage 4, rather than during stages 2 and 3. As a result, the judgment of experts on HIT adoption rates and trends tends to be lower than what the HIMSS-Dorenfest database or other survey-based studies report.

The estimates of adoption developed in this report reflect whether a provider organization (e.g., hospital or physician office) has just purchased a HIT application by signing a contract with a vendor or has an application already installed. The sum of these two measures, in percentages, shows the share of healthcare providers that are committed to implementing a HIT application. For our purposes, this sum is the preferred measure of adoption, because it best reflects the level of commitment to HIT adoption and factors associated with it, and it helps to better identify the organizations that have not yet made a purchase decision. Such measures of adoption are estimated for various HIT applications based on HIMSS-Dorenfest data.

Estimated Adoption of Major Clinical HIT System Components

The HIMSS-Dorenfest database surveys provider organizations on whether or not they have installed a particular HIT system or have just signed a contract with a vendor or developer of the software to buy such a system. We include the newly contracted HIT systems in our estimate of policy-relevant adoption, although the "installed" category better reflects the commonly held meaning of *adoption.*

The database directly measures adoption of ambulatory[1] EMR and inpatient CPOE, but it does not measure ambulatory CPOE. Although the survey does not have a category for an EMR System (EMR-S) in hospitals, it measures numerous clinical HIT hospital applications, some of which are the major components of any EMR-S:

- CPR: Computerized Patient Records
- CDS: Clinical Decision Support
- CDR: Clinical Data Repository.

For the purposes of this analysis, we determined that the basic inpatient EMR-S would be expected to include these components, which need to be integrated into one system. The functionality of an EMR-S depends on the functionality and interoperability of these and additional components, such as outcomes and quality measurement applications, CPOE, and PACS. The composition of a typical EMR-S is illustrated with a description of a system from St. Jude Children's Research Hospital (SJCRH) quoted here:[2]

---

[1] Technically, the database includes only ambulatory facilities that are owned or managed by IHDSs.

[2] See http://www.dcpress.com/frolick2.htm

The Components of the Electronic Record: OCF, PowerChart, and Discern Expert

The electronic medical record system at SJCRH has several components. The Open Clinical Foundation (OCF) is the repository at the center of the new electronic medical record. The OCF is an Oracle database that stores clinical and administrative information. This new database functions as a data warehouse and has the ability to group information based on any one particular patient parameter. For example, patient clinical outcomes with regard to a particular protocol can easily be grouped and presented by the electronic medical records system, thus eliminating the need for data managers to collect the information manually.

PowerChart is the graphical user interface that caregivers access at the clinical workstation. It is composed of two parts: the Organizer and the Chart. The Organizer allows the user to quickly check for new patient test results immediately after logging onto the system. In addition, it allows the user to indicate which test results they have reviewed. The Chart is the electronic form of the patient medical record. It is through this interface that the user can review clinical lab results, nurses' notes, physicians' notes, and patient demographics. Features that are available in the Chart such as the problem list, visit list, and growth chart also allow caregivers to track a patient's medical progress. This electronic medical record makes gathering patient information more efficient because it automatically groups similar data together.

Discern Expert is a program that evaluates best clinical practice criteria and monitors events in the system for compliance. It is part of a decision support system that assists healthcare providers at the point of care by linking historical patient data with current clinical data and assessing that data based on built-in clinical rules. Historically, work in clinical decision support systems has been concentrated on designing alerts and reminders for physicians[;] however[,] more recent systems are focused on overall compliance with patient care plans (Broverman, 1999). A "starter set" of rules was developed in Discern Expert for the lab, radiology, pharmacy, PowerChart, admitting/registration, and the Chart modules (Milli project scope document, 1998). Managing patient care through the use of decision support systems ultimately means that a patient's quality of care improves.

Thus, one measurement of inpatient EMR that we use requires a hospital to have CPR, CDR, and CDS. For this analysis, the upper bound of an EMR estimate does not require these components to be from the same vendor, whereas the lower bound of inpatient EMR requires that all three come from the same software vendor to ensure integration. In addition, we have a "partially-integrated EMR" measure, according to which CPR and CDR have to be provided by the same software vendor. We recognize that many organizations may have interfaced these components from different vendors' software in a way that allowed a level of integration; however, that information was not captured in the HIMSS-Dorenfest database.

The HIMSS-Dorenfest database can produce more-or-less generalizable esti-mates for hospital adoption, because it accounts for the majority of U.S. community hospitals, including about 90 percent of non-profit, 90 percent of for-profit, and 50 percent of government-owned (non-federal) hospitals. However, it excludes hospitals that have less than 100 beds and are not members of healthcare systems, which underrepresents small rural hospitals.[3] Thus, we adjusted EMR and CPOE adoption rates by accounting for lower adoption rates in the providers that were not captured in the HIMSS-Dorenfest database: We assumed that adoption rates are about one-quarter lower[4] in the nonrepresented hospitals in each ownership category and weighted ownership categories to derive adoption rates for the true community-hospital population. We used size categories to adjust PACS adoption for the entire hospital population, because hospital size seems to be the most important factor in the adoption of such a system.

The final estimate of inpatient EMR upper-bound adoption in community acute care hospitals is around 30 percent, and the estimate for partially integrated EMR is about 25 percent. These estimates must be treated as an upper bound even for a basic EMR-S, because the decision support or patient record components of such a system may be limited to individual departments or have limited functions.

As for ambulatory settings, the HIMSS-Dorenfest database covers a little less than a quarter of the U.S. physicians practicing in office settings. Because it covers only those practices that are owned, leased, or managed by hospitals or integrated healthcare systems, the HIMSS-Dorenfest sample is biased toward larger practices that may have access to the technology through their parent organizations. Assuming that practice size is the major driving factor of EMR adoption, we weighted the adoption rates in the practices of different sizes by the true distribution[5] in the physi-cian population to arrive at the adoption rate per practice and per physician in Table 2.1 (see Chapter 3, Factors That Influence HIT Adoption in Ambulatory

---

[3] Technically, the HIMSS-Dorenfest database covers all the community acute care hospitals that are larger than 100 beds and all other facilities, including smaller hospitals (less than 100 beds), chronic care facilities, and ambulatory practices, that belong to the same healthcare system as the hospital.

[4] This adjustment is primarily based on the lower HIT adoption in hospitals smaller than 100 beds, and on the fact that HIMSS-Dorenfest database underrepresents those hospitals. It captures only about one-third of those hospitals smaller than 100 beds, but over 90 percent of larger hospitals. The difference between average adoption in the HIMSS-Dorenfest database sample and adoption in smaller hospitals is around 25 percent.

[5] True distribution of the physician practices by size was derived from the American Medical Association (AMA), *Physician Socioeconomic Statistics* (2003) and from the AMA, *Medical Group Practices in the US* (2002). The estimates of adoption rates for the corresponding distribution derived from the HIMSS-Dorenfest database were adjusted to account for the true distribution of the physician practices by size.

Table 2.1
Raw and Adjusted Estimates of Clinical HIT Adoption

Technology Adopted	HIMSS-Dorenfest		Population-Adjusted		
	Installed	Adopted	Installed	Adopted	Adopted per Bed/per MD
Partially Integrated Inpatient EMR	21%	27%	20%	25%	28%
Upper-Limit Inpatient Basic EMR	26%	32%	25%	30%	34%
Inpatient CPOE	10%	17%	9%	15%	17%
Radiology PACS	28%	36%	23%	30%	43%
Ambulatory EMR	13%	17%	9%	12%	17%

Clinics section). Because these adoption rates are projected from hospital-affiliated physician rates, they likely represent an upper bound of adoption estimates.

We also estimated the adoption of HIT per ambulatory physician and per hospital bed, to get a crude estimate of the share of patient and physician population *exposed* to HIT technology (which is not the same as *adoption* on the user level, because it does not guarantee that every doctor in a hospital with HIT will use it for every case).

Clinical information technology systems in hospitals include a wide variety of applications above and beyond basic EMR and CPOE. A majority of the hospitals have already adopted such clinical HIT "basics" as Master Patient Index, Order Communication and Results, Clinical Documentation software, and Clinical Data Repository. Most hospitals also have HIT applications for managing medical records, including Dictation, Transcription, Chart Locator, Encoder, and Abstracting. Other HIT applications are earlier in their diffusion process—with relatively lower adoption rates: Electronic Medicine Administration Record (17 percent), Point of Care (Bedside Monitoring) software (41 percent), and Medical Record Imaging (37 percent).[6]

Over 80 percent of all hospitals also have basic IT systems in their radiology, laboratory, and pharmacy departments, including medicine-dispensing software applications. However, except in surgical and emergency departments, adoption of other departmental information systems—such as information systems in critical care, cardiology, and, especially, obstetrical systems—is much lower. In contrast,

---

[6] These adoption rates are not adjusted for the non-Dorenfest population. They would be a little lower if they had been.

PACS have gained in popularity in recent years: In the first half of 2004, 36 percent of acute hospitals were committed to adopting radiology PACS; 27.5 percent had already installed the system; and 8.5 percent had signed a contract to buy a system. Adoption of cardiology PACS is lower, only about 9 percent (7 percent having installed the system and 2 percent having signed a contract). See Table 2.1.

The level of sophistication and breadth of a hospital HIT system can be measured as a combination of a basic inpatient EMR and CPOE, PACS, and other clinical HIT applications (see Figure 2.1). While the adoption of basic EMR is around 32 percent, only 14.5 percent has both a basic EMR system and radiology PACS, and only 9 percent has EMR adopted together with CPOE. Only about 5.5 percent of hospitals has already adopted (installed or contracted) the three important clinical HIT applications: EMR, PACS, and CPOE. Only one out of every 20 hospitals (or even less, accounting for hospitals not included in the HIMSS-Dorenfest survey) has an EMR-S that contains digital radiology images and has physician order entry with all the decision support capabilities.

Figure 2.1
Adoption of Basic EMR, Combined with Other Clinical HIT Applications

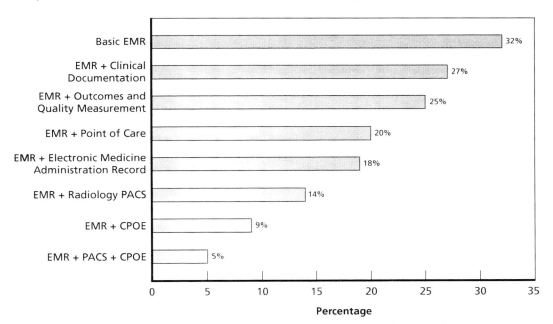

SOURCE: Estimated from the HIMSS-Dorenfest database (HIMSS, 2004) sample, non-adjusted.
RAND *MG409-2.1*

Dynamics of the HIT Diffusion Process

The HIMSS-Dorenfest survey (2004, second release) contains adoption dates, so we were able to construct diffusion curves for major clinical HIT applications (Figure 2.2). These diffusion curves represent the cumulative percentage of adopters in any given year, based on the year when the application was contracted for, as reported by the organization. For inpatient EMR, which we measure as consisting of CPR, CDS, and CDR, we used the year when its last component was contracted for.

Since only about two-thirds of the adopters reported the contract date, we have extrapolated the adoption date for the remaining one-third to correspond to the reported pattern of diffusion, assuming that the missing data follow the same pattern. Therefore, our extrapolation may introduce a slight bias, if those who did not report the contract date did adopt predominantly in the early years rather than proportionally to those who reported. We display the diffusion curves beginning in 1990, when the estimated adoption levels were around 1 percent. The curve ends at year-end 2003, based on available data at the time of this analysis.

Figure 2.2
Diffusion of Inpatient EMR, CPOE, and PACS, and of Ambulatory EMR Systems

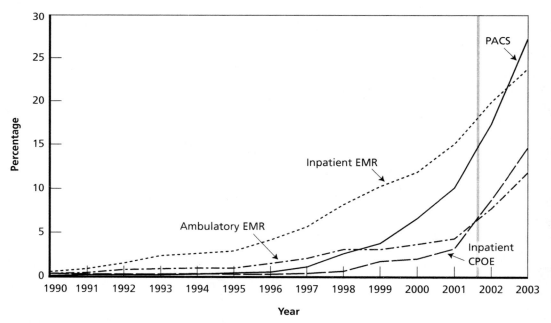

NOTE: The shaded vertical line illustrates a suggested shift for the curves to reflect the "have it in place" measure of adoption.

Because very few hospitals report the actual date of installing the HIT application, we were unable to generate the diffusion curves for the date when the system was installed in the hospital, rather than the date it was contracted for. The average difference between the date of contract and the date of automation is about a year and a half, with longer periods in the early years and shorter periods recently. Thus, if someone is particularly interested in the diffusion of HIT systems based on the date of installation, it could be approximated by shifting the contract-based diffusion curve one or two years to the right. (The dashed vertical line in Figure 2.2 illustrates a suggested shift of each of the curves to the right until the dashed line becomes the year 2003, to reflect the "have it in place" measure of adoption.)

The diffusion curves were constructed from the HIMSS-Dorenfest respondents, and then adjusted downwards to reflect lower adoption in the rest of the hospital population, based on estimates in the preceding section, Estimated Adoption of Major Clinical HIT Systems Components (see Figure 2.2).

Inpatient EMR (or, at least, its upper-limit measure) has the slowest acceleration, in relative terms (if one compares the time to change from 5 to 10 percent; the Inpatient curve is the slowest) of diffusion in recent years, and would probably take the longest to diffuse. In contrast, ambulatory EMR diffusion appears more dynamic since 2000, despite its slow start. Although Radiology PACS achieved 5 percent diffusion almost five years later than inpatient EMR, it exceeded EMR diffusion in 2002. From the years 2000 to 2003, the CPOE adoption level increased sevenfold, which might be caused by unprecedented policy attention to the role of CPOE in reducing medical errors. If this is the case, then this rapid start does not reflect the natural diffusion pattern and might be overly optimistic.

HIT-Adoption Estimates from Alternative Sources

In comparison with most other reports (see Table 2.2), our HIT-adoption estimates ("this report") are reasonably conservative.

Our estimates are considerably lower than the HIMSS survey of Corporate Information Officers (CIO; HIMSS Leadership Survey, 2004b) results on HIT (EMR) adoption in healthcare facilities[7]: up to 56 percent, at least twice as high as

---

[7] Of respondents, 86 percent represents hospital settings; the rest is physician offices and chronic care facilities.

Table 2.2
HIT-Adoption Rates in the Alternative Surveys

Alternative Survey	Inpatient EMR		CPOE		Ambulatory EMR	
	Installed	Adopted	Installed	Adopted	Installed	Adopted
This report	20%–25%	25%–30%	9%	15%	9%	12%
HIMSS, 2004b	19%–56%	>56%				40%
MRI, 2004	21%–42%		17%		21%–42%	
Modern Physician, 2003						>42%
MGMA, 2004					20%	<40%
Deloitte, 2002					<13%	
Leapfrog, 2004			4%	<20%		

NOTE: The numbers in the table should not be compared directly without reference to the text, because the definition of the HIT systems and the sampling vary significantly among the surveys.

our estimate of 20 to 30 percent. This 56-percent estimate includes the following stages of EMR implementation:

- 19 percent has a fully operational system
- 37 percent has begun installation
- 23 percent has developed a plan to implement in the future.

We suspect that the main reason the HIMSS surveys report a higher level of adoption is the bias in the sample of providers. Responding to the HIMSS survey is voluntary, and the selection of potential respondents is neither comprehensive nor random. Response rates were around 20 percent in the CIO survey and 9 percent in the physician survey (HIMSS, 2004a, b). The organizations represented are more likely to be those with IT leadership, because they are more likely to be interested in this survey and respond to it. The total number of respondents is relatively low: about 200 physicians and practice managers in the ambulatory HIT survey (HIMSS, 2004a), and 300 CIOs of healthcare facilities in the other survey (HIMSS, 2004b). In both surveys, the size of the hospitals/physician practices is biased toward larger facilities. Another explanation for the high estimates of HIT adoption in the HIMSS CIO survey is that CIOs reported the EMR adoption in their organization (often a healthcare system), not necessarily in *each* healthcare facility of their organization. Thus, if the CIO of a large IHDS knows that there is an EMR in one of the IHDS's six hospital facilities, he might have answered yes to the question on whether his organization implemented an EMR.

The latest annual survey by the Medical Records Institute (MRI) reports on the adoption of various HIT/EMR functions in 2004. The respondents were invited by email broadcasts to fill in the survey on their website. Thus, MRI authors warn against extrapolating the reported adoption levels to all U.S. healthcare providers, owing to response bias. One of the functions reported in the MRI (2004) report is close to our definition of a *basic EMR:* a Clinical Data Repository (CDR) that supports storage of EMR data; text codes and reimbursement codes, which had an adoption rate of 42.2 percent in use at the beginning of 2004, and an additional 15 percent for planned use in the next year (2005). About 21 percent of the respondents claimed that their CDR also supports clinical codes, such as SNOWMED, a clinical code standard; another 25 percent plans to have this system in use within a year. In addition, the survey shows that over 90 percent of hospitals with an EMR-S also have it available in their outpatient departments—a result that can be extrapolated to our HIMSS-Dorenfest–based estimates. MRI surveyed over 400 respondents, but it is difficult to identify which segment of healthcare their estimates represent, since the survey lumps together organizations and users within organizations, hospitals and physician offices, integrated systems, and home care services, and includes non-U.S. providers as about 15 percent of its sample.

The HIMSS *Survey of Ambulatory Technology* (2004a) claims that 39 percent of the practices it surveyed has an EMR, including:

- 24 percent that has an EMR in all departments
- 15 percent that has an EMR in some departments.

Another 36 percent planned to buy an EMR in 2004. This percentage is several times higher than our estimate of 12 percent among practices or 17 percent among physicians.

The Deloitte *Research Survey on Physician Use of IT* (Miller et al., 2004), conducted in ambulatory practices at the end of 2001, was a relatively well-designed phone-interview study on HIT adoption of a national, stratified random sample of 1,200 physicians. Despite a low response rate of about 6 percent, the sample of respondents presents a wide range of demographic characteristics and specialties. According to this study, 13 percent of respondents reported use of EMR, although the study notes it might be an overestimate, due to a response bias and physicians' broad definition of *an EMR.* Taking into account these considerations and the fact that the survey was conducted in 2001, we believe that our estimate of 12 percent for EMR adoption at the beginning of 2004 is comparable.

According to an annual survey by *Modern Physician*/PriceWaterhouseCoopers (PWC), conducted in 2003, 42 percent of physician practices already invested in an EMR and another 15 percent was planning to invest in one within a year. A total of 80 percent planned to invest by 2005. The generalization of these numbers to the entire physician-practice population is questionable, since the results are based on a Web-based survey, which physicians were invited to complete on the *Modern Physician* website. This method clearly introduces a substantial response bias, because the website is viewed disproportionately more by HIT adopters, who are also more inclined to answer a survey on HIT use and adoption.

A preliminary finding from the 2004 MGMA [Medical Group Management Association] Survey of EMR adoption in physician group practices indicates that about 20 percent of members have an *electronic medical record,* defined as a system that is accessible through a computer terminal and stores medical and demographic information in a relational database. In addition, fully 40 percent of those surveyed indicated that they would implement an EMR System within the next two years. An additional 8 percent of MGMA respondents indicated that they had a system that could combine electronically stored physician notes from dictation and transcription with paper charts scanned into an electronic document-imaging system, and 3 percent had a system just with scanned documents. These estimates represent adoption in practices with three or more physicians, and they are a little higher than our HIMSS-Dorenfest–based estimate (unadjusted) for practices with two or more physicians, which shows 14 percent of the practices having an EMR in place and another 4 percent having a contract to install one. MGMA estimates are also based on an email survey limited to MGMA members and group practices, which may introduce a response bias.[8]

As for CPOE adoption, the recent Leapfrog survey (2004) reports that 4 percent of hospitals fully implemented[9] CPOE in 2003, and another 16 percent will have it implemented by 2006. In total, 20 percent of hospitals will have CPOE fully implemented by 2006.

Our estimates show that about 7 percent of hospitals has CPOE in place (although not necessarily fully implemented), and another 9 percent has contracted for it, implying that at least 16 percent will have a CPOE system fully implemented in 2006 (if it takes 1-1/2 years from contracting to full adoption). Another 3 to 5 percent of hospitals that contracted for CPOE in 2004 may not have been captured in the survey yet, which makes our estimates practically identical to Leapfrog's.

The MRI survey in 2004 also provides a recent estimate of CPOE that all kinds of providers have in use today—11 to 17 percent, depending on whether these are pharmacy, lab, or radiology order systems—and another 28 to 32 percent is going to install the system within a year.

The HIMSS-Dorenfest database also contains some data on CPOE use on the user level in organizations, showing that, among 7.8 percent of hospitals with CPOE in place, only 15 percent (1.3 percent of the total) mandates CPOE use, and only 40 percent (3.5 percent of the total) uses CPOE to enter all orders (including prescriptions, labs, diagnostic, and patient care).

---

[8] More-representative estimates may be derived from a random sample of 16,000 groups. The groups will be mailed paper surveys, and the MGMA data were to have been available by March 2005.

[9] The Leapfrog definition of a *fully implemented CPOE system* is as follows: Prescribers enter at least 75 percent of all medication orders via a CPOE system.

The 3.5 percent of hospitals that enters most of their orders through CPOE approximate what conventionally is meant by "fully implemented," and is equivalent to the adoption rate of 3.5 to 4 percent cited in the Leapfrog study.

Also, about 50 percent of those IHDS with CPOE in some of their hospitals has over 50 percent of physicians using it (a much higher rate than on the hospital level, because a system may include some hospitals with CPOE and some without).

There are many other sources of HIT-adoption data, but all have design flaws and response problems similar to those of the sources already cited. So far, the data from the HIMSS-Dorenfest database appear to have the highest quality and to be the most representative of clinical HIT adoption in hospitals and integrated healthcare delivery systems, despite their shortcomings, such as the absence of a well-established measurement of an inpatient EMR system. The definitions of clinical HIT applications, such as *inpatient CPOE* and *outpatient EMR* in HIMSS-Dorenfest, are not ambiguous. However, our working definition of *an EMR* as CPR+CDS+CDR represents an upper bound of functionality rather than a realistic estimate of the technology in use.

Surveys on the Factors That Enhance or Create Barriers to HIT Adoption

Although the aforementioned surveys and studies fail to deliver clear or reliable estimates of HIT adoption, they are quite useful for forming hypotheses on causes of the difference in adoption among different types of healthcare providers, through the reported enhancers of and barriers to HIT adoption.

The MRI survey (2004) lists the top motivating factors for adoption of an EMR System in ambulatory and hospital settings. The motivations of over 75 percent of the hospitals include the need to

- share patient-record information among healthcare practitioners and professionals
- improve clinical processes or workflow efficiency
- reduce medical errors; improve patient safety
- improve quality of care.

Over half of the hospitals also mentioned the need to

- facilitate clinical decision support
- improve clinical data capture

- provide access to patient records at remote locations
- improve clinical documentation to support appropriate billing service levels.

Over 75 percent of ambulatory practices are mostly motivated to adopt an EMR System by the need to

- improve clinical processes or workflow efficiency
- improve quality of care
- improve clinical documentation to support appropriate billing service levels.

Over half of them also quote the need to

- share patient-record information among healthcare practitioners and professionals
- reduce medical errors; improve patient safety
- provide access to patient records at remote locations
- improve clinical data capture
- establish a competitive advantage
- contain or reduce healthcare costs
- meet the requirements of legal, regulatory, or accreditation standards
- facilitate clinical decision support.

We might expect that those hospitals and practices for which these motivations matter the most would be the first to adopt EMR Systems. Hospitals and practices that participate in the multi-provider local system might be more likely to adopt, because they are motivated to share records among the participating providers. Ambulatory practices that face heavy competition might hurry to adopt EMR Systems to improve their competitiveness, although for hospitals this factor is a little less important, according to the survey. However, these factors indicate possible policy levers to speed the adoption process.

The MRI report (2004) also provides information on the perceived barriers to EMR System adoption and implementation, lumping together hospital and ambulatory respondents. The majority of respondents mentioned the lack of adequate funding or resources as a barrier to adopting an EMR System, confirming the conventional wisdom and opinion of the experts on this subject. The same barrier tops the list in the HIMSS survey. We should expect that provider organizations with limited capital and smaller organizations would lag in adoption of EMR Systems because of the large fixed cost of such an investment.

Other major barriers that were indicated in both the MRI and HIMSS surveys include

- lack of support from medical staff
- difficulty in finding an EMR solution that is not fragmented among vendors or IT platforms
- lack of quantifiable return on investment (ROI).

CHAPTER THREE

Factors Related to HIT Adoption

In this chapter, we estimate the current level and pattern of HIT adoption in the different types of healthcare organizations, and we evaluate factors that affect this diffusion process. By comparing adoption rates across different types of healthcare providers and geographical areas, we help focus the policy agenda by identifying which healthcare providers lag behind and may need the most incentives to adopt HIT. Next, we employ regression analysis to separate the effects of the provider's characteristics and factors on adoption of Electronic Medical Records (EMR), Computerized Physician Order Entry (CPOE), and Picture Archiving Communications Systems (PACS), and compare the effects to findings in the literature.

Method

To analyze the HIT-adoption pattern in various types of hospitals and office practices, we used the HIMSS-Dorenfest database and AHA survey of hospitals to answer two questions: "What types of hospitals are less likely to adopt HIT?" and "Which factors may influence the adoption of HIT?"

Our analysis focused on major clinical HIT systems, which were defined and measured in the preceding chapter: inpatient and outpatient EMR, CPOE, and radiology PACS. The differences in the effects of various factors on EMR, versus CPOE or PACS, provide additional insights on the incentives that drive adoption of different kinds of HIT.

The source of data on adoption factors is the HIMSS-Dorenfest database for the beginning of 2004, which covers nearly 4,000 acute care community hospitals in the United States (three-quarters of the total number) and most physician practices owned by hospital systems. The HIMSS-Dorenfest dataset also includes basic demographic information at the hospital level and some detailed characteristics of the hospital systems, such as financial characteristics and revenues by payer. We merged this dataset with the AHA dataset (2002), which contains detailed demographic information at the hospital level. A total of 3,640 observations were merged successfully, although about 500 of them had missing observations for most of the AHA data.

Because of the structure of HIMSS-Dorenfest data, all absolute HIT-adoption rates reported in this chapter apply only to the hospitals or physician practices owned or managed by systems or to hospitals that are larger than 100 beds. The rates cannot be generalized to the entire hospital or physician practice population. However, with caution, relative differences among them can be applied to the rest of the population.

The Pattern of HIT Adoption in For-Profit as Opposed to Non-Profit Hospitals

Our research shows that the pattern of HIT adoption differs substantially between for-profit and non-profit hospitals. EMR and PACS adoption rates in for-profits are as low as half the rate of adoption in non-profit hospitals, and CPOE adoption is one-fifth the rate of adoption in non-profit hospitals. The dynamics of their adoption also differs: Since 2001, non-profits have accelerated adoption of clinical HIT, and particularly EMR, whereas for-profits' adoption has stagnated. Non-profits also have a much higher percentage of new contracts for acquiring clinical HIT systems: Of non-profit hospitals, 8 percent currently have contracted for an EMR, 12 percent for CPOE, and 9 percent for PACS; for-profits have contracted for such systems at the rate of 2, 2, and 4 percent, respectively.

However, for-profits are ahead in adoption of other IT applications that assist with hospital management and improve efficiency, such as Executive Information Systems, Managed Care Contract Management software, Enterprise Resource Planning software, and Time and Attendance software. For-profit's higher adoption of Outcome and Quality Measurement application stands in contrast to its lower adoption of clinical systems; but the description of the functionality of this application includes "measuring and analyzing the hospital performance, costs and efficiency of care provided," all of which are helpful in managing profitability. Table 3.1 demonstrates the distribution of the clinical and managerial HIT applications and systems.

There is also a considerable difference in the IT budget in for-profit and non-profit hospitals. For example, hospitals with very high HIT budgets are mostly non-profit: only 0.5 percent of for-profit hospitals and hospital systems spends over 4 percent of its operating budget on IT, whereas 8 percent of non-profit hospitals does so. However, more for-profit hospitals are making significant budget commitments to HIT; 41 percent of for-profits have 3 to 4 percent of their budgets spent on IT, whereas the corresponding number for non-profits is only 22 percent. These findings

Table 3.1
Adoption of HIT Applications and Systems in For-Profit and Non-Profit Hospitals

	HIT System or Application	For-Profit	Non-Profit
Non-Profit Hospitals Lead in:	CPOE	4%	21%
	Obstetrical Information Systems	6%	17%
	E-Medication Administration Record	9%	20%
	Integrated EMR	11%	20%
	Premium Billing	15%	26%
	Partially Integrated EMR	18%	29%
	Radiology PACS	18%	41%
	Basic EMR (CPR+CDS+CDR)	25%	34%
	Medical Record Imaging	26%	41%
	Computerized Patient Record	40%	58%
	Patient Scheduling	62%	73%
For-Profit Hospitals Lead in:	Enterprise Resource Planning	26%	14%
	Eligibility	38%	30%
	Intensive Care	40%	32%
	Point of Care application	45%	40%
	Outcomes and Quality Management	70%	57%
	Clinical Decision Support	65%	58%
	Executive Information Systems	77%	59%
	Managed Care Contract Management	72%	60%
	Clinical Data Repository	70%	63%
	Clinical documentation	72%	65%
	Time and Attendance	94%	84%

may suggest that some pioneering non-profits are investing heavily to adopt new and expensive HIT systems; for-profits might be catching up in building a HIT infrastructure. We need longitudinal data on the dynamics of HIT acquisition and spending to really understand the origins of these differences and the degree to which they represent high start-up costs versus ongoing maintenance costs.

Our findings regarding differences in adoption are consistent with findings in the literature, but the reasons for these differences are not perfectly clear. One study (Parente and Van Horn, 2003) reports that for-profit and non-profit hospitals adopt clinical IT in order to achieve different outcomes: For-profits are reducing costs and lengths of stay, and non-profits are trying to increase the quality and quantity of the services they provide. This result implies that for-profit hospitals do not yet expect major clinical IT (EMR and, especially, CPOE) to substantially reduce their costs and improve efficiency, and that non-profit hospitals adopting clinical HIT are being guided by considerations other than efficiency improvement. To the extent that these implications are true, different sets of policies may need to be crafted to stimulate adoption in these two groups.[1]

Hospital Type

According to Table 3.2, the real leaders in the HIT-adoption process are academic and pediatric hospitals. Adoption of major HIT systems in academic hospitals is up to two times higher than that in nonacademic hospitals, although this relationship is partially determined by other factors, such as larger size. The fact that pediatric hospitals have much higher adoption rates might be explained by a higher relative benefit of using EMR and CPOE while caring for children (i.e., children are not as reliable a source of their medical histories, medications, etc., as are adults), and by the fact that a major multi-hospital pediatric system happened to be a leader in EMR system adoption.[2]

Critical access hospitals have very low adoption rates, possibly because of their tiny size and rural location. They also typically offer a limited range of services, with the more-complex cases being stabilized and transferred to larger facilities. Thus, low adoption in these hospitals may suggest that the perceived benefits of HIT are lower

Table 3.2
Adoption in Acute Care Hospitals of Various Types

Hospital Type	No. of Hospitals in Category	Percentage Adopting		
		Basic EMR	CPOE	Radiology PACS
Long-Term Acute	110	10%	1%	3%
Critical Access	76	13%	16%	18%
General Medical	55	16%	11%	22%
General Medical & Surgical	3,235	31%	15%	35%
Academic	343	44%	28%	59%
Pediatric	116	54%	46%	53%

[1] For-profit hospitals may increase adoption when clinical IT is developed enough to improve efficiency of care delivery or when incentives are realigned so that they allow hospitals to reap the benefits of improvements in quality and efficiency of their healthcare services. On the other hand, non-profit hospitals are very likely to adopt clinical systems just because "this is a right thing to do" if they have organizational capacity and financial resources for them; therefore, subsidies or organizational help for the needy non-profit hospitals might be helpful.

[2] The Shriners' system of hospitals for children developed an EMR and CPOE information system and began the installation process in all 20 of its hospitals in 2004.

in such a setting. Long-term acute[3] care hospitals, as a category, have the lowest HIT adoption. The reasons for such a dramatic difference are unclear, but we know that long-term care hospitals are much smaller in size and, until very recently, were exempt from the Medicare prospective payments system, which was historically an important driver in increasing HIT adoption according to Borzekowski (2002a).

Size and Rural Status of the Hospital

Experts in the trade literature have often reported that small size of a hospital or medical practice was the major predictor of low HIT adoption. Our analysis supports this qualitative statement, showing around a 10-percent positive correlation between adoption of an EMR System and various measures of a hospital's size: staffed hospital beds, number of full-time equivalent personnel, number of patients admitted, patient-days, etc. Among the variables that reflect the size of a hospital, annual hospital operating costs have the highest correlation with HIT adoption: 13 percent for EMR and 20 percent for CPOE. The size of a hospital is more important in predicting the adoption of a PACS, showing up to a 33-percent correlation with the number of beds. The difference in adoption between smaller and larger hospitals is reasonable: non-profit hospitals with more than 100 beds have up to a 1.5-times-higher adoption rate of EMR and CPOE and over a 2-times-higher adoption rate of PACS than hospitals with less than 100 beds (see Figure 3.1). For-profit hospitals demonstrate a conflicting relationship of HIT adoption with size: Those larger than 100 beds have lower EMR adoption than in the smaller hospitals, but much higher PACS adoption (up to 3 times higher than hospitals with fewer than 100 beds). Since the type, location, and other characteristics of a hospital affect its size, we cannot directly attribute the entire relationship to size.

Rural status is another widely quoted factor related to the lower adoption of HIT. According to our data analysis, the difference in EMR adoption between urban and rural locations is relatively small: 33 percent versus 29 percent. These relationships might be stronger if we included smaller stand-alone hospitals that are omitted in the HIMSS-Dorenfest survey. However, the difference between rural and urban hospitals is much more vivid in adoption of CPOE (13 percent versus 19 percent) and, especially, PACS (22 percent versus 42 percent).

---

[3] This is a separate category from chronic long-term hospitals, which were not considered in this analysis.

Table 3.3
Correlations of Alternative Measures of Hospital Size with Clinical HIT Adoption

Size of the Hospital	Sample *N*	Basic EMR	CPOE	PACS
Beds staffed in acute facility	3,634	10%	10%	34%
Annual operating costs	863	13%	20%	35%
Admissions in acute facility	3,634	10%	12%	35%
Inpatient-days	3,634	9%	11%	32%
FTE personnel	3,634	11%	17%	34%
Surgical operations	3,555	9%	12%	31%
Outpatient visits	3,634	7%	19%	31%

NOTE: All correlations are significant at the .05 level.

Figure 3.1
HIT Adoption by AHA Hospital-Bed-Size Category

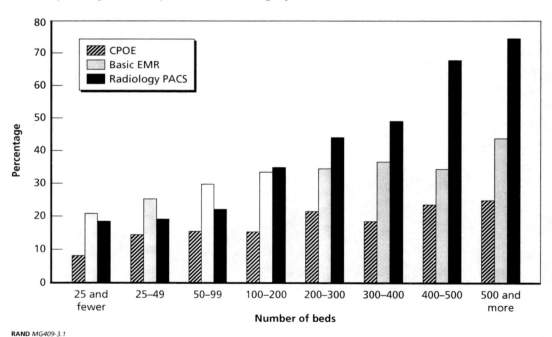

RAND *MG409-3.1*

Medicare and Medicaid

The share of Medicare seems to be a considerable factor in the adoption of clinical HIT. One-third of the community hospitals have the majority of their patients' claims paid by Medicare, and they are less likely to have major clinical HIT systems than are other hospitals (see Figure 3.2): The relative difference between them ranges from 30 percent for basic EMR to 100 percent for a PACS. The magnitude of correlation for this relationship is comparable with the effect of hospital size and shows up in each of a number of different measures of Medicare share: Medicare admissions, patient-days, and, especially, revenues. Although the negative relationship between high Medicare share and HIT adoption persists regardless of the profit status of the hospital, it is much stronger in non-profit hospitals—e.g., the correlation with having an EMR is four times larger in non-profit hospitals. Also, higher share of Medicare is correlated with a later adoption date of CPOE and PACS.

In contrast to Medicare, a high share of Medicaid does not have a clear association with a lower adoption of clinical HIT. Indeed, the share of Medicaid patient admissions has a weak positive correlation with clinical HIT adoption, whereas the share of Medicaid patient-days has a weak negative relationship. Figure 3.3 demonstrates that those hospitals with more than 25 percent of their patients on Medicaid have a little higher adoption rate than those with less than 25 percent of their patients on Medicaid. Medicaid share measured as a percentage of the hospital

Figure 3.2
Clinical HIT Adoption in Hospitals with a Majority or a Minority of Medicare Patients

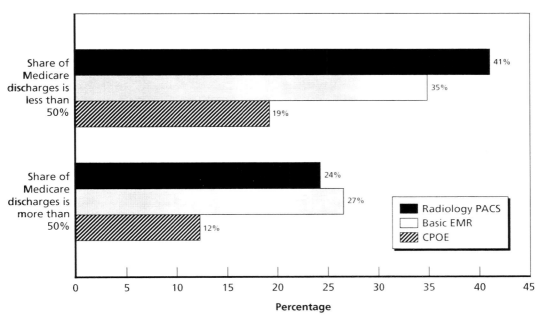

Figure 3.3
Clinical HIT Adoption in Hospitals by Share of Medicaid Patients

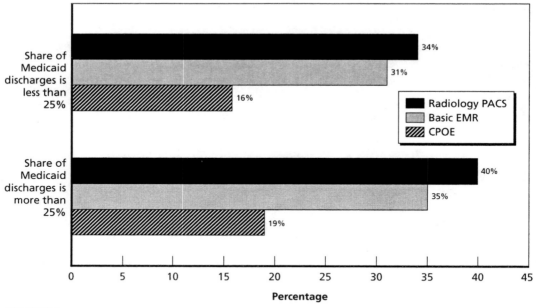

revenue[4] has a small positive correlation with adoption of EMR and CPOE. We assumed that lower reimbursement rates of Medicare compared with other insurers explained, at least in part, its negative effect on hospitals' investment in HIT; and we were surprised to see that Medicaid share did not show the same effect for the same reasons (Table 3.4).

This ambiguous relationship is partially explained by the fact that academic hospitals treat a large share of Medicaid patients. Another explanation is the high share of managed care among Medicaid patients, which positively affects HIT adoption.[5] In addition, we hypothesize that hospitals with a large share of Medicaid

---

[4] This relationship is derived from only 970 freestanding hospitals. The HIMSS-Dorenfest database provides data on the sources of revenue at the level of a hospital system or stand-alone hospital. We can evaluate the relationship between various types of revenue and adoption by limiting the results to stand-alone hospitals and single-hospital systems.

[5] Medicaid managed care and Medicare managed care have a positive relationship with HIT adoption, whereas Medicaid and Medicare from traditional sources have a negative relationship. This analysis is based on Californian hospitals (Office of Statewide Health Planning and Development [OSHPD] financial dataset for the year 2003, http://www.oshpd.cahwnet.gov/HQAD/Hospital/financial/hospAF.htm). Medicaid in California has a larger share of managed care than does Medicare.

Table 3.4
Correlations of Alternative Measures of Medicare and Medicaid Share with Clinical HIT Adoption

Share of Medicare and Medicaid	Sample *N*	Basic EMR	CPOE	PACS
Percentage of Medicare inpatient-days	3,634	**–6%**	**–9%**	**–5%**
Percentage of Medicaid inpatient-days	3,634	–1%	–1%	**–4%**
Percentage of Medicare discharges	3,634	**–14%**	**–14%**	**–17%**
Percentage of Medicaid discharges	3,634	3%	–1%	4%
Percentage of Medicare revenues	754	**–10%**	**–14%**	**–11%**
Percentage of Medicaid revenues	754	5%	6%	**–4%**

NOTE: Correlations that are significant at the .05 level are highlighted in **bold**.

patients are generally considered disadvantaged and often receive grants and other financial help, which could be devoted to HIT investment (i.e., these are likely to be publicly financed hospitals that do not depend primarily on fee-based revenue for their operating budgets).

The lower HIT-adoption rate in hospitals with a larger share of Medicare patients suggests the importance of Center for Medicare and Medicaid Services (CMS) involvement in HIT policies. This result raises the expectation that hospitals with a larger share of Medicare patients would be interested in the potential efficiency savings promised by HIT. With Medicare patients, DRG reimbursement that creates risk-sharing means that hospitals may keep the savings associated with shorter stays, and HIT can help to achieve reduced resource utilization.

Indeed, the research by Borzekowski (2002a,b) has reported that the introduction of the prospective payment system for Medicare has speeded the adoption of early hospital information systems. Despite this apparent incentive, there could be factors, such as capital constraints related to a higher share of Medicare and its relatively lower reimbursement levels when compared with commercial patients, causing the delay in the adoption of HIT in these hospitals.

Managed Care Status

Managed care is definitely a factor in HIT adoption, although the precise relationship is elusive because of measurement problems. The AHA survey measures managed care by asking whether a hospital or the healthcare system to which that hospital belongs has an equity interest in health maintenance organization (HMO) or preferred provider organization (PPO) insurance products. Although it is likely that hospitals that accept many managed care patients have their own managed care plan, this measure may not properly reflect the share of revenues that comes from managed care sources.

Healthcare providers that own some share of a managed care insurance product constitute about one-quarter of the community hospitals and include systems such as Kaiser Permanente and Intermountain Healthcare. Figure 3.4 demonstrates that HMO or PPO hospitals and systems have considerably higher adoption of clinical HIT than do those hospitals with no equity interest in either an HMO or a PPO. These differences are more marked between for-profit hospitals than between non-profit hospitals, indicating the possible role of managed care (as a competitive threat) as an added incentive for for-profits to gain efficiency improvement through HIT.

An alternative measurement of managed care involvement—whether or not a hospital derives any revenue from capitated payments (Table 3.5)—shows that capitated hospitals have considerably higher HIT adoption. The share of these revenues has a strong positive correlation only with CPOE adoption; the relationship with EMR System adoption is a weak and negative one. The data available for stand-alone hospitals[6] also show that having a high share of managed care revenue—in

Figure 3.4
Equity Investment in HMO or PPO by Hospital or Hospital System, and by Clinical HIT Adoption

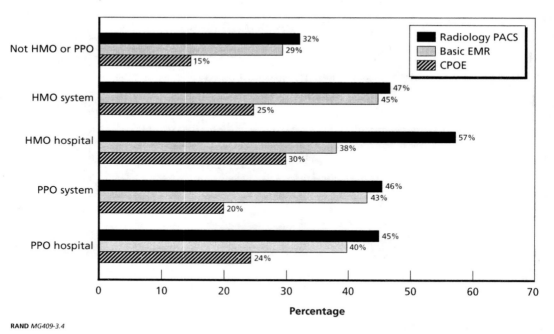

RAND MG409-3.4

---

[6] The HIMSS-Dorenfest database provides data on the sources of revenue at the level of a hospital system or a stand-alone hospital. We can evaluate the relationship between various types of revenue and adoption by limiting the results to stand-alone hospitals and single-hospital systems.

Table 3.5
Correlations of Alternative Measures of Managed Care with Clinical HIT Adoption

Measure	Sample *N*	Basic EMR	CPOE	PACS
Percentage of capitated revenues	2,729	1%	**11%**	**4%**
Percentage of risk-shared revenues paid on risk-shared basis	2,678	**4%**	**4%**	**5%**
Percentage of capitated revenues, if >0	422	0%	**17%**	–3%
Percentage of risk-shared revenues, if >0	348	3%	3%	4%
No. of lives under capitated payments	1,776	–2%	**11%**	**5%**
No. of lives under capitated payments, if >0	340	–6%	**20%**	4%
Percentage of revenues from managed care in the subsample of single hospitals	754	**7%**	**11%**	**14%**

NOTE: Correlations that are significant at the .05 level are highlighted in **bold**.

particular, from HMOs and point of service (POS) plans—increases the probability of adopting EMR and, especially, CPOE systems.

Our project's literature review and site visits reinforced our sense that fully integrated and budgeted delivery systems, such as Kaiser, Group Health, and the Veterans' Administration (VA) system have high EMR System adoption rates. But the HIMSS-Dorenfest data may be too diffuse and too hospital system–oriented to identify these strong associations. For less-integrated systems, managed care contracts from capitated delivery systems may pay hospitals on a per-diem basis, providing less incentive for HIT-enabled restructuring for efficiency. Nevertheless, even the weaker affiliation in the HIMSS-Dorenfest and AHA data between managed care and adoption somewhat supports the opinion of experts that having a captive patient population in a closed HMO system would internalize the benefits of healthcare quality improvement and stimulate HIT adoption.

System-Level Factors and Regional Factors

A number of findings may support the importance of *network externalities* (i.e., the value of technology investment for the provider depends on whether other providers have adopted this technology) in the decision to adopt HIT. The majority of community hospitals belong to multi-hospital systems; thus, their adoption behavior is related to their system's adoption behavior (see Table 3.6). We found, through HIMSS-Dorenfest data, that clinical HIT adoption by other hospitals from the same multi-hospital system is the single-largest determinant of whether or not the hospital adopts an EMR System, with a correlation 8 times stronger than the frequently cited correlation with the hospital size. This result may indicate that

Table 3.6
Correlations of the Adoption Rate in Other Hospitals from the Same System or MSA with Clinical HIT Adoption

Measure	Sample N	Basic EMR	CPOE	PACS
Adoption percentage among other hospitals from same system	2,588	77%	85%	17%
Adoption percentage among other hospitals from same MSA	2,337	15%	25%	12%

NOTE: All coefficients are significant at .05 level.

- a HIT-adoption strategy is determined more by the system than by an individual hospital
- when a HIT system is deployed to all hospitals in a system, economies of scale may result, decreasing the costs of the system for each individual hospital
- hospitals derive additional benefits from having a similar system in the networked hospitals
- the sharing of HIT-adoption experiences is beneficial.

If the link between adoption in the system and hospital adoption can be proven to be causal, it is clearly important for policy to target those 200 multi-hospital systems that have not adopted EMR Systems in any of their hospitals. However, the spread of the HIT-adoption experience to other hospitals within the system can be expected in the very near future, since 70 percent of the systems' hospitals belong to one of those multi-hospital systems that already have EMR in some of their hospitals.

Another curious fact is that smaller multi-hospital systems have higher adoption of clinical HIT than do larger ones: The difference between systems with fewer than five hospitals and those with more than five hospitals is about 1.5 times (see Figure 3.5). The probability of HIT adoption in an individual hospital generally falls as the number of hospitals in a hospital system increases, which may indicate that the investment might become more difficult to coordinate as the hospital system gets larger.

About 15 percent of all community hospitals are managed[7] rather than owned or leased by the systems. These contract-managed hospitals have half the HIT-adoption rate of owned hospitals (see Figure 3.6). This difference is partially explained by the fact that contract-managed hospitals are about half the size of owned hospitals, are predominantly rural, and are often government-owned. Thus, they may have insufficient administrative capacity. Additionally, many non-profit hospitals enter into

---

[7] Under contract-management, a hospital's board of trustees retains an outside organization to manage the facility, and, usually, that organization also makes decisions on HIT investments.

Figure 3.5
HIT Adoption Among Hospitals That Belong to Smaller or Larger Hospital Systems

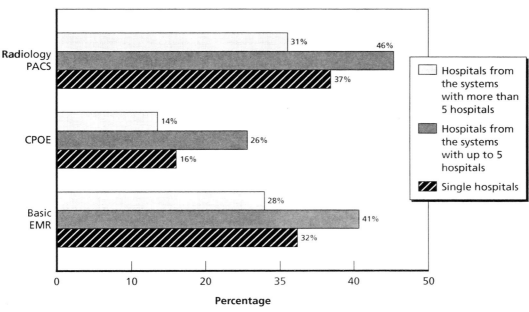

management contracts as a strategy for coping with tough fiscal constraints, which is likely a major barrier to HIT adoption (Carey and Dor, 2004, p. 194).

Additional characteristics of healthcare systems available from the AHA database are the type of system, based on the degree of differentiation and centralization of its services, physician arrangements, and insurance products among the member hospitals. HIT adoption is highest in systems that have highly centralized physician arrangements and insurance products at the system level, with less centralized delivery of the healthcare services. These systems are predominantly non-profit, have a small number of hospitals, and their hospitals are close to each other. As one would expect, the laggards in HIT adoption are independent hospital systems[8] and decentralized hospital systems.

Over a third of system-owned hospitals belong to decentralized hospital systems, which offer highly differentiated services and insurance products and may lack an overarching structure for coordination. These systems have a large number of hospitals spread over a broad geographic area. It may be that smaller, more localized hospital systems may have higher adoption rates because they may better benefit from coordination of patient care and a common strategy for HIT investment. They

---

[8] *Independent hospital systems* are largely horizontal affiliations of independent hospitals.

Figure 3.6
HIT Adoption in Contract-Managed Hospitals

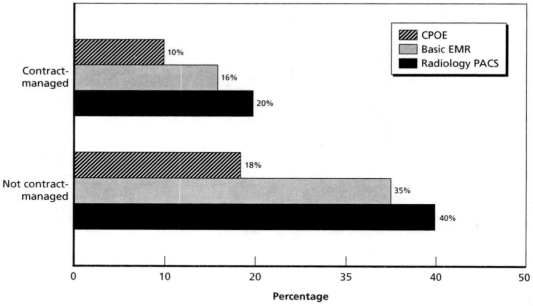

RAND *MG409-3.6*

may also have a much stronger network effect (i.e., a hospital derives additional benefits from having EMR adopted by the rest of the hospital network) from affiliated hospitals in the same locale that treat the same patient populations. See Figure 3.7.

Another finding that adds to the network-externality argument is that hospital HIT adoption is related to the adoption by other hospitals from the same metropolitan area, with correlations of 15 percent for EMR and 25 percent for CPOE systems (see Table 3.6). Also, adoption of EMR and CPOE does not necessarily increase with the size of the metropolitan area: It peaks in the midsize cities (see Figure 3.8). Quite possibly, relatively small markets are more suitable for organization and coordination of information exchange, which increases benefits from HIT for the next adopter. Also, when there are fewer hospitals in the area, hospitals and their systems are likely to treat the same patients more than once and will need their clinical histories.

Figure 3.7
HIT Adoption in Healthcare Systems (HS) of Different Types

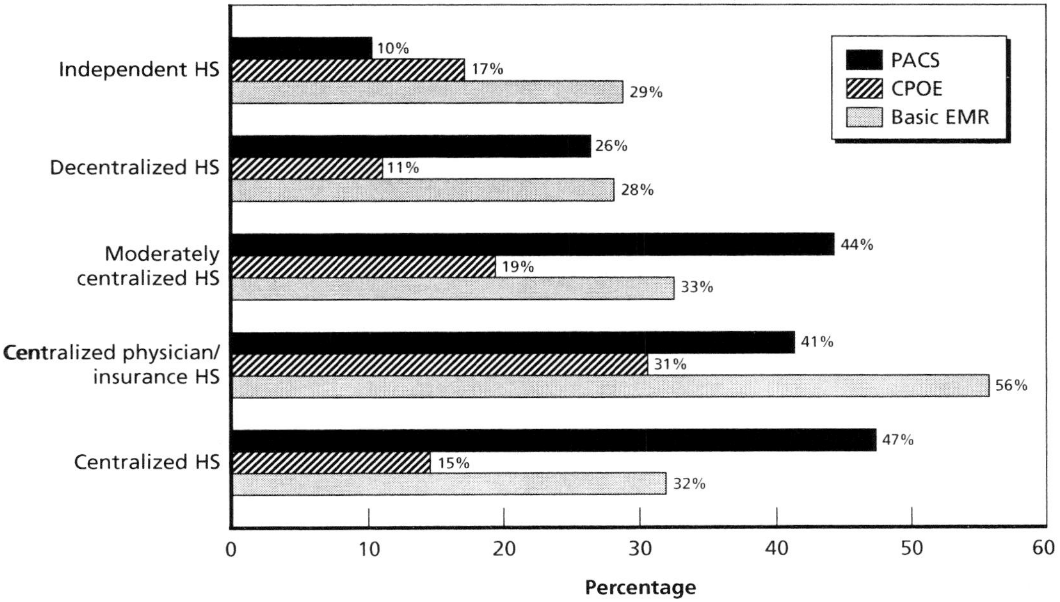

Competition

The degree of competition[9] in the market (inversely, its concentration) has the opposite effect on EMR adoption in for-profit versus non-profit hospitals, possibly providing them with different incentives. Non-profit hospitals are more likely to have EMR and CPOE when their market is more competitive. For for-profits, the correlation is twice as strong, but in the opposite direction: For-profits tend to adopt EMR more when their market is less competitive, although there is no such effect for CPOE. At the same time, high competition in the market substantially increases the probability of a PACS adoption in both non-profit and for-profit hospitals, which may indicate that PACS is universally viewed as an investment that enhances the competitiveness of any given hospital. See Figure 3.9.

_____

[9] The inverse of competitiveness is measured by the Hirschman-Herfidahl Index (HHI) of market concentration, which is equal to the sum of each hospital's squared market share (based on hospital beds) divided by hospitals within a hospital market. The market is measured as a radius that covers 75 percent of a hospital's admissions. The competition is higher when HHI is lower, indicating that there are more hospitals in the market and that their market shares are more even.

Figure 3.8
Size of the Metropolitan Area and HIT Adoption

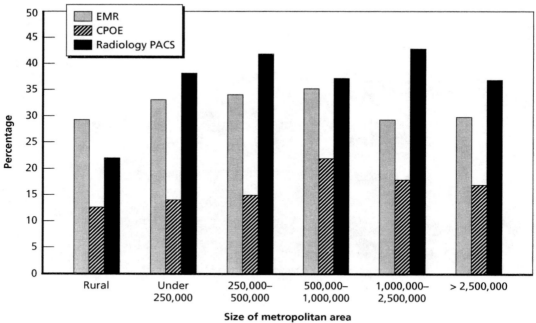

One suggestion is that non-profits may compete on the quality and prestige that the EMR System may deliver, whereas for-profits may substitute clearer ROI-driven investments when the market pressure is higher. Alternatively, for-profits may have more-independent physician-staffing arrangements, increasing the complexity of making and implementing an adoption decision. But, in truth, these are mostly speculations and undoubtedly oversimplify the issues involved. More research on the effects of tax status and competition could help us understand the real incentives behind different HIT adoption and lead to grounded policies that promote HIT adoption through competition.

Community and Quality Orientation of the Hospital

The AHA survey includes questions on the hospital's mission, community, quality-related efforts, and scope of services provided (Table 3.7). The analysis of that data against HIT adoption reveals the relationship of HIT adoption to quality improvement, although it is difficult to determine the direction of causality (i.e., whether HIT affects quality or vice versa). HIT adoption is positively related to the quality orientation of the non-profit hospitals, such as self-assessment against

Figure 3.9
Correlation of HIT Adoption with the Index of Market Concentration (the Inverse of Competition), by the Profit Status of the Hospital

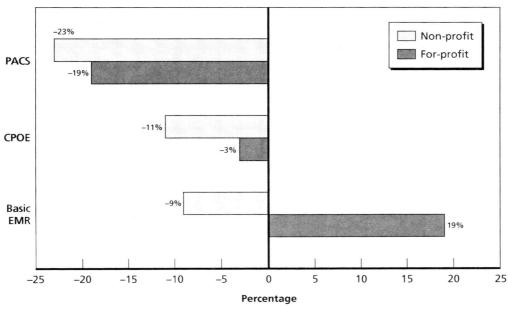

RAND *MG409-3.9*

Table 3.7
Correlations of Endogenous Variables with Clinical HIT Adoption

Variable/Measure	Sample *N*	Basic EMR	CPOE	PACS
Average length of stay	3,634	**–8%**	**–5%**	**–8%**
FTE per adjusted admission	3,634	**–7%**	0%	**–4%**
Nurses-to-MDs ratio	2,498	**9%**	**14%**	**20%**
Community-orientation score	2,746	**8%**	**6%**	**10%**
Quality-orientation score	2,876	**10%**	**7%**	**14%**

NOTE: Correlations that are significant at the .05 level are highlighted in **bold**.

Baldridge-like criteria for sustained continuous improvement, and dissemination of reports on quality. This finding could suggest that incentives to implement quality initiatives and to improve and report quality would drive up HIT adoption. Also, hospital systems that provide a wide array of community-oriented services, such as community outreach, health fairs, community health screenings, case-management, and health information services are more likely to have clinical HIT.

Another interesting observation is that EMR, CPOE, and, especially, PACS adoption is higher when the ratio of nurses to doctors in the hospitals is higher. Also, we observed a modest positive relationship between FTE per admissions and EMR adoption, and a modest negative relationship between LOS and EMR, and EMR tenure, which may indicate a certain efficiency gain from EMR Systems, although an elaborate model is required to capture the causality in this relationship.

Link to Primary Care

Hospitals that have primary care departments and, especially, hospitals that have primary care locally in their hospital system have higher rates of clinical HIT adoption (see Figure 3.10). It is possible that the need for information exchange between a hospital and its related primary care departments would stimulate the adoption of clinical HIT.

Figure 3.10
Adoption in Systems and Hospitals with a Primary Care Department

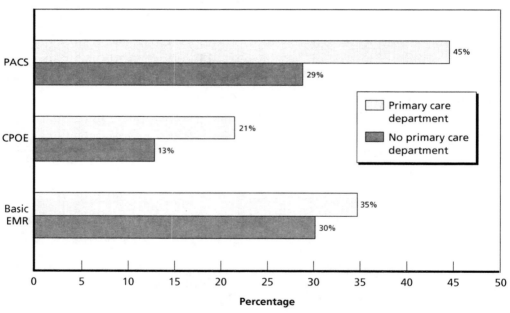

Factors That Influence HIT Adoption in Ambulatory Clinics

Our data on ambulatory practices are limited to those practices that are owned by healthcare delivery systems, which constitute less than one-fourth of office-based physicians in the United States.

The characteristics of the ambulatory clinics in the HIMSS-Dorenfest database are limited mostly to their size and type. The size effect is very important in the ambulatory clinics: Practices with over 30 physicians are 3 times as likely to adopt an EMR System as is a solo practitioner (see Figure 3.11).

EMR-adoption rates also vary by the type of ambulatory practice. The leaders in EMR adoption are multi-specialty clinics, with an EMR-adoption rate of 33 percent—more than 2 times higher than adoption in single-specialty practices or primary care practices. Multi-specialty clinics are large: They account for only 10 percent of all practices, yet they cover over 40 percent of the office-based physician population. Thus, their size and, consequently, their larger organizational and financial resources may explain the higher adoption rate, as well as the fact that there is greater organizational value to be derived from exchanging information among doctors in multi-specialty clinics.

Figure 3.11
Adoption of HIT in Physician Practices, by Size

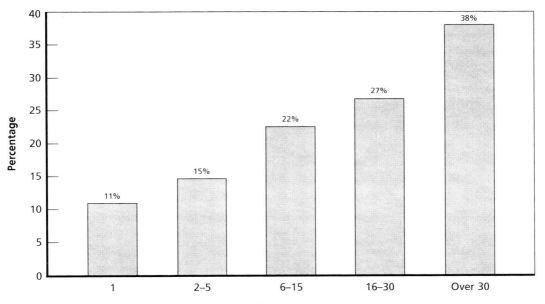

Adoption in any given ambulatory practice owned by an integrated healthcare delivery system is most related to the adoption rate in the rest of the system: The correlation reaches 97 percent, which is even higher than the corresponding relationship for the hospitals. This result demonstrates that investment in ambulatory EMR might be decided on and paid for at the level of the system and determined by the characteristics of the system, and/or it might have a higher value for the practice because of its connectivity within a system. Alternatively, there might be a measurement failure, with the reported adoption of ambulatory EMR at the IHDS level not reflecting the actual adoption patterns of the practice sites associated with the IHDS.

A similar argument applies to the positive relationship between EMR adoption in a hospital and in its affiliated ambulatory practice, where adoption in the practice affiliated with the EMR-equipped hospitals is twice as high as in practices affiliated with hospitals not equipped with EMR.

There is also a significant correlation between an ambulatory EMR adoption by the clinic and a high share of managed care revenues in the affiliated hospital system (see Figure 3.12): The correlation with HMO revenues reaches 60 percent. However, these high correlations may partially result from the fact that ambulatory EMR is mostly adopted by the parent IHDS, and correlations on the level of practices

Figure 3.12
Correlation of Ambulatory EMR Adoption Rate in a Healthcare System, with the System's Revenues Derived from Various Sources

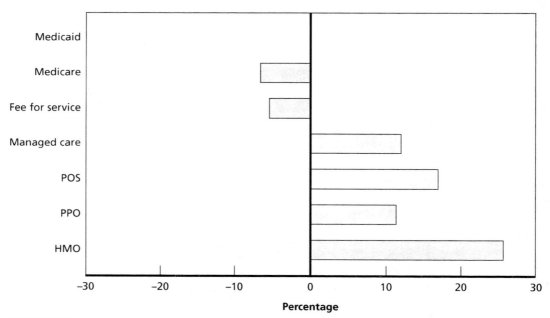

might be spurious. Thus, we aggregated ambulatory EMR-adoption rates at the IHDS level. What we obtained is a little weaker correlation, but with the same direction of effect. As with hospitals, a high share of Medicare revenues (but not Medicaid revenues) is associated with reduced ambulatory EMR adoption in the healthcare system. Managed care, and especially HMO share, is strongly correlated with EMR adoption.

Multivariate Regression Analysis for HIT Adoption in Acute Care Hospitals

To assess the incremental relationships of major clinical HIT systems' adoption and various organizational and market factors, we used probit regression analysis. Because we discovered markedly different HIT-adoption behavior between for-profit and non-profit hospitals, we also did separate regressions for each of these categories. The pooled regression (see Table 3.8) proves that for-profit hospitals have significantly lower adoption of EMR, CPOE, and PACS than do non-profit hospitals, even when all other major organizational characteristics—such as size, rural location, academic, pediatric, or contract-managed status, share of Medicare and Medicaid, and HMO

Table 3.8
Robust Probit Regressions with Basic Independent Variables in Acute Care Hospitals

Hospital Type or Characteristic	EMR	CPOE	PACS
Log of adjusted admissions (size)	0.038***	0.013*	0.122***
For-profit	−0.088***	−0.158***	−0.210***
Rural	0.049**	0.003	−0.078***
Government-owned	0.002	−0.018	−0.006
Academic status	0.061*	0.093***	0.128***
Pediatric	0.172**	0.256***	0.143*
Contract-managed	−0.154***	−0.048**	−0.044
Percentage of Medicare admissions	−0.247***	−0.204***	−0.063
Percentage of Medicaid admissions	−0.108	−0.247***	−0.035
HMO hospital	−0.044	0.044	0.105**
HMO system	0.068**	0.051**	−0.025
PPO hospital	0.077**	0.040	−0.001
PPO system	0.053*	−0.016	0.092***
N	2,983	2,983	2,983
P-value for the Wald test	0	0	0

NOTES:
Coefficients are presented in terms of marginal change in the probability of adoption.
*Coefficient is significant at the .10 level.
**Coefficient is significant at the .05 level.
***Coefficient is significant at the .01 level.

and PPO status—have been controlled for. Moreover, for-profit status is the largest among the binomial effects for CPOE and PACS adoption. Even though in this regression most other independent variables have effects similar to those discovered in univariate analysis, it might be more useful to discuss their effects separately for for-profit and non-profit hospitals.

In the non-profit regressions, the size of a non-profit hospital remains a highly significant positive factor for EMR adoption and, especially, for PACS adoption. However, CPOE adoption seems to be independent of size. Rural location makes no significant difference in EMR or CPOE adoption, possibly because we control for the smaller hospital size typical of rural hospitals. However, rural hospitals have a significantly lower probability of PACS adoption. See Table 3.9.

As in the pooled regression, academic status in non-profit hospitals remains a highly significant positive factor. However, an alternative measure of teaching status—trainees per staff—shows a negative relationship with EMR adoption when academic status is controlled for (Table 3.10). Pediatric status has a consistently significant positive effect on the adoption of EMR, and, especially, CPOE, but not on PACS adoption. Share of Medicare admissions decreases the probability of EMR and CPOE adoption. Because we controlled for other factors, such as academic status, the share of Medicaid no longer has a positive correlation with HIT adoption; it has a negative effect similar to that of Medicare, statistically significant for EMR and CPOE.[10] The research by Parente and Van Horn (2003) derives similar results for adoption of patient care IT systems: a high percentage of Medicare and Medicaid patients or revenues decreased the probability of adopting a patient care information system. This finding may suggest that a high share of Medicare and Medicaid patients decreases availability of such quality-enhancing HIT as EMR and CPOE, possibly through tighter budgets or different priorities imposed by CMS on the hospitals.

However, it is difficult to explain why PACS does not have a significant negative relationship with Medicare and Medicaid share, unlike EMR and CPOE. Also, it is unclear why contract-managed hospitals have significantly lower chances of having EMR or CPOE, but not PACS. This difference may indicate that adoption of PACS is driven by different incentives and considerations than is adoption of EMR and CPOE, such as the presence of measurable ROI.

The effects of the variables that capture different types of managed care involvement by the hospital or its system vary, depending on the type of HIT system. We found that non-profit hospital systems with an equity interest in PPO or HMO are significantly more likely to adopt EMR, whereas a system's equity interest in an

---

[10] The effect becomes larger and more significant when we use an alternative measure of Medicaid: share of Medicaid inpatient-days.

Table 3.9
Robust Probit Regressions for Non-Profit Acute Care Hospitals

Hospital Type or Characteristic	EMR	CPOE	PACS
Log of adjusted admissions (size)	0.036***	0.010	0.100***
Rural	0.027	0.016	−0.121***
Academic status	0.131***	0.133***	0.120**
Trainees per staff	−1.358**	−0.180	1.076*
Pediatric	0.241**	0.304***	−0.066
Contract-managed	−0.121***	−0.099***	0.017
Percentage of Medicare admissions	−0.382***	−0.246***	−0.196
Percentage of Medicaid admissions	−0.274**	−0.337***	−0.040
HMO hospital	−0.039	0.098**	0.120**
HMO system	0.070**	0.060*	−0.053
PPO hospital	0.108**	0.053	0.021
PPO system	0.048	−0.026	0.083**
Member of healthcare system	0.102**	0.027	0.005
Number of hospitals in a system	0.000	0.000	−0.001**
N	*1,710*	*1,710*	*1,710*
P-value for the Wald test	*0*	*0*	*0*

NOTES:
Coefficients are presented in terms of marginal change in the probability of adoption.
*Coefficient is significant at the .10 level.
**Coefficient is significant at the .05 level.
***Coefficient is significant at the .10 level.

Table 3.10
Alternative Estimates from Robust Probit Regressions for Non-Profit Acute Care Hospitals When Quality Score Is Included

Hospital Type or Characteristic	EMR	CPOE	PACS
Log of adjusted admissions (size)	0.045***	0.015	0.123***
Rural	0.045*	0.008	−0.056**
Academic status	0.101***	0.110***	0.083**
Trainees per staff	−1.155**	0.031	0.932*
Pediatric	0.155*	0.295***	0.137*
Contract-managed	−0.137***	−0.086***	0.012
Percentage of Medicare admissions	−0.357***	−0.228***	−0.105
Percentage of Medicaid admissions	−0.172*	−0.249***	−0.036
HMO hospital	-0.048	0.060*	0.100**
HMO system	0.077**	0.028	−0.042
PPO hospital	0.103***	0.047	−0.009
PPO system	0.048	−0.015	0.091**
Member of healthcare system	0.025	0.040**	0.053**
Number of hospitals in a system	0.000	0.001**	−0.001*
Quality-orientation score	0.023**	0.008	0.021*
N	*1,630*	*1,630*	*1,630*
P-value for the Wald test	*0*	*0*	*0*

NOTES:
Coefficients are presented in terms of marginal change in the probability of adoption.
*Coefficient is significant at the .10 level.
**Coefficient is significant at the .05 level.
***Coefficient is significant at the .10 level.

HMO, but not a PPO, increases the probability of adopting CPOE. PACS adoption is positively affected by a hospital's equity in an HMO, and by a system's equity in a PPO. Finally, membership in a hospital system increases the chances that a non-profit hospital will adopt an EMR System, but not a CPOE or PACS.

Market competition appeared to be an insignificant factor in all of the regression specifications, and it was not included in the final analysis.[11] It is likely that competitiveness of the market is related to such factors as rural location and size, and that the correlation of adoption with competition disappears when those factors are controlled for.

However, the quality-orientation score is a significant and positive factor in the adoption of EMR and PACS, when all other hospital characteristics have been controlled for. Since the quality score is likely to be endogenous to the adoption of HIT, we included this variable in a separate regression analysis (Table 3.10).

As expected, the characteristics of for-profit hospitals have quite different relationships to HIT adoption (see Table 3.11). For example, size is not a significant variable for EMR and CPOE adoption, although it is significant and positive for PACS, similarly to non-profits. Rural location has a surprisingly positive, and highly significant, effect on EMR adoption, and it has an expected negative effect on the adoption of PACS. Because of a smaller sample size and a low variation in the independent variables, we could not assess all the factors in every for-profit model, and the regression model of CPOE adoption is only marginally significant according to the Wald test. The effects of the teaching/academic status (to the extent of their availability) are similar to those for non-profit hospitals. However, unlike non-profits, being a contract-managed hospital does not have any significant negative effect on HIT adoption in the for-profit hospitals. Also, Medicare share has a significant negative effect only on EMR adoption, and Medicaid share does not have any significant effect. Managed care variables do not have a significant effect on HIT adoption. Unlike for non-profits, the number of hospitals in a system has a significant negative effect on EMR adoption, as does membership in a system for CPOE. Finally, membership in a hospital system increases the chances that a for-profit hospital will adopt CPOE or a PACS.

The analysis we performed reinforces the idea that adoption of EMR or CPOE by for-profit hospitals is driven by considerations and incentives other than those that drive their non-profit peers. Nevertheless, those characteristics of hospitals that matter for adoption of radiology PACS are fairly similar, despite the large differences in adoption rates.

---

[11] We have not included the regressions with a competition variable, because this variable has a large number of missing observations, reducing the sample size and resulting in having to drop other variables.

Table 3.11
Robust Probit Regressions for For-Profit Acute Care Hospitals

Hospital Type or Characteristic	EMR	CPOE	PACS
Log of adjusted admissions (size)	0.007	−0.002	0.109***
Rural	0.215***	0.005	−0.091***
Academic status	N/A	0.656***	0.204
Trainees per staff	4.033*	N/A	−19.895**
Contract-managed	0.221*	N/A	−0.025
Percentage of Medicare admissions	−0.284*	−0.033	0.198
Percentage of Medicaid admissions	0.079	−0.023	0.116
HMO hospital or system	−0.027	N/A	0.030
PPO hospital or system	−0.106*	0.070**	0.003
Member of healthcare system	0.095	−0.085*	−0.071
Number of hospitals in a system	−0.002***	0.0005	0.0005*
Sample size	386	313	390
P-value of Wald test	0.0000	0.077	0.0001

NOTES:
Coefficients are presented in terms of marginal change in the probability of adoption.
*Coefficient is significant at the .10 level.
**Coefficient is significant at the .05 level.
***Coefficient is significant at the .01 level.
N/A = impossible to estimate because of collinearity issues or the variable predicts failure perfectly.

CHAPTER FOUR

Summary of Results and Conclusions

Certain results may be the most useful for HIT policymaking. We summarize those results in this chapter.

The overall EMR adoption rate, as defined by having made a contractual commitment to adopt, is between 20 and 30 percent for hospitals and up to 12 percent for physician practices. Further, the overall rate of adoption is growing, especially in non-profit healthcare organizations. Our analysis supports earlier findings that the pattern of HIT adoption differs drastically from for-profit to non-profit hospitals. Not only is the adoption of major clinical HIT systems, such as EMR, CPOE, and PACS, significantly lower in for-profits, even when we control for other factors, but hospital and system characteristics and market factors, such as competition, also have different effects on HIT adoption. These differences suggest that the largest barriers to adoption may be other factors, such as the business case, not the lack of access to capital. Further, policy options designed to stimulate widespread HIT adoption must include incentives that galvanize both for-profits and non-profits.

We also found that smaller non-profit hospitals with a high share of Medicare and Medicaid patients or that are contract-managed have significantly lower adoption of EMR and PACS. Small ambulatory practices are particularly slow adopters of ambulatory EMR, which may suggest that smaller provider organizations, the organizations with disproportionate shares of government-pay patients, and those under financial stress may need special policy consideration. Policies could be designed to improve the business case for HIT adoption and could potentially include incentives or targeted subsidies. Measures could be taken to improve smaller organizations' ability to successfully adopt HIT. The negative relationship between HIT adoption and a high share of Medicare and Medicaid from traditional payment sources also suggests that there is a role for CMS in developing policies to stimulate HIT adoption.

Managed care, particularly HMOs, increases the probability of adopting EMR and CPOE, which may suggest that policies containing managed care–type incentives would be helpful in stimulating adoption of clinical HIT systems. Managed care seems to be particularly important for ambulatory EMR adoption.

The strong evidence that HIT adoption spreads within a short time across integrated healthcare delivery system suggests that a potential target for policy incentives is the corporation rather than individual providers.

References

American Hospital Association (AHA), Annual Survey Database, Chicago, Ill., Fiscal Year 2002.

American Medical Association (AMA), *Medical Group Practices in the US,* Chicago, Ill., 2002.

American Medical Association, *Physician Socioeconomic Statistics,* Chicago, Ill., 2003.

Borzekowski, R., "Health Care Finance and the Early Adoption of Hospital Information Systems," Washington, D.C.: Discussion Paper No. 2002-41, Finance and Economics Discussion Series from the Board of Governors of the Federal Reserve System (U.S.), 2002a.

Borzekowski, R., "Measuring the Cost Impact of Hospital Information Systems: 1987–1994," Washington, D.C.: Board of Governors of the Federal Reserve System, September 2002b. Available at http://ideas.repec.org/p/fip/fedgfe/2002-42.html (accessed March 2005).

Carey, K., and A. Dor, "Trends in Contract Management: The Hidden Evolution in Hospital Organization," *Health Affairs,* Vol. 23, No. 6, November/December 2004.

Conn, J., "More Practices Adopting Electronic Health Records: Survey," *Modern Physician,* January 25, 2005 (describes the results of MGMA Survey, 2004).

Deloitte, Research Survey on Physician Use of IT (same as Miller et al., 2004).

Healthcare Information and Management Systems Society (HIMSS) Analytics^{SM} Database (formerly the Dorenfest IHDS+TM Database), second release, 2004. (Referred to as "the HIMSS-Dorenfest database" in the text.)

HIMSS, *Survey of Ambulatory Technology,* Chicago, Ill., February 9, 2004a. Report available at http://www.himss.org/content/files/ambulatory_tech_survey_0209.pdf.

HIMSS Leadership Survey, *Healthcare CIO Results: Final Report,* Chicago, Ill., February 23, 2004b. Report available at http://www.himss.org/2004survey/docs/Healthcare_CIO_final_report.pdf (accessed March 2005).

Leapfrog Survey Press Release, available at http://www.leapfroggroup.org/media/file/Leapfrog-Survey_Release-11-16-04.pdf (accessed March 2005).

Medical Records Institute (MRI), *Medical Records Institute's Sixth Annual Survey of Electronic Health Record Trends and Usage for 2004.* Available at http://www.medrecinst.com/pages/latestNews.asp?id=115; accessed January 2005.

MGMA [Medical Group Management Association] Survey, 2004 (summarized in Conn, 2005).

Miller, R. H., J. M. Hillman, and R. S. Given, "Physician Use of IT: Results from the Deloitte Research Survey," *Journal of Healthcare Information Management,* Vol. 18, No. 1, Winter 2004, pp. 72–80.

Modern Physician, *Sixth Annual Modern Physician/PricewaterhouseCoopers Survey of Executive Opinions on Key Information Systems Issues.* Can be purchased through *Modern Physician* website: http://www.modernphysician.com/mediaindex.cms?type =surveys&topic=Technology.

Parente, S. T., and J. L. Dunbar, "Is Health Information Technology Investment Related to the Financial Performance of US Hospitals? An Exploratory Analysis," *International Journal of Healthcare Technology and Management,* Vol. 3, No. 1, 2001, pp. 48–58.

Parente, S. T., and L. Van Horn, "Hospital Investment in Information Technology: Does Governance Makes a Difference?" working paper, 2003. Available from http://misrc.csom.umn.edu/workshops/2003/fall/Parente_111403.pdf (accessed March 2005).

Solovy, A., "The Big Payback: 2001 Survey Shows a Healthy Return on Investment for Info Tech," *Hospitals and Health Networks,* July 2001, pp. 40–50.

Wang, B., D. Burke, and T. Wan, "Factors Influencing Hospital Strategy in Adopting Health Information Technology," paper presented at 2002 Annual Research Meeting, Health Services Research: From Knowledge to Action, Washington, D.C., June 23–25, 2002.